Great Artists
Salvador Dalí

ABDO
Publishing Company

Adam G. Klein

visit us at
www.abdopublishing.com

Published by ABDO Publishing Company, 4940 Viking Drive, Edina, Minnesota 55435.
Copyright © 2007 by Abdo Consulting Group, Inc. International copyrights reserved in all
countries. No part of this book may be reproduced in any form without written permission from
the publisher. The Checkerboard Library™ is a trademark and logo of ABDO Publishing
Company.

Printed in the United States.

Cover Photo: Getty Images
Interior Photos: AP/Wide World pp. 5, 19, 25; Art Resource pp. 12, 21; Bridgeman Art Library
    pp. 11, 17, 27; Corbis pp. 1, 15, 20, 23; Getty Images pp. 4, 9, 13, 29

Salvador Dalí art images pp. 5, 11, 12, 13, 15, 17, 19, 21, 23, 27, 29 © 2006 Salvador Dalí, Gala-
    Salvador Dalí Foundation / Artists Rights Society (ARS), New York.

Series Coordinator: Megan M. Gunderson
Editors: Rochelle Baltzer, Megan M. Gunderson
Cover Design: Neil Klinepier
Interior Design: Dave Bullen

3 9082 10428 8199

Library of Congress Cataloging-in-Publication Data

Klein, Adam G., 1976-
    Salvador Dalí / Adam G. Klein.
        p. cm. -- (Great artists)
    Includes index.
    ISBN-10 1-59679-728-2
    ISBN-13 978-1-59679-728-4
    1. Dalí, Salvador, 1904---Juvenile literature. 2. Artists--Spain--Biography--Juvenile
literature. 3. Surrealism--Spain--Juvenile literature. I. Dalí, Salvador, 1904- II. Title.

N7113.D3K54 2006
709'.2--dc22

2005048325

Contents

Salvador Dalí

Salvador Dalí was a painter, a sculptor, and a filmmaker. He designed jewelry and furniture, too. Dalí based much of his work on personal interests, which adds a **unique** quality to his art. His unusual style made him one of the most recognizable artists of his day.

Most people remember Dalí as a Surrealist. He used Surrealism to make his life into a work of art. In the process, a legend was created.

Both Dalí and his art were **controversial**. Still, even people who did not like his work admired his talent. Dalí simply wanted people to be shocked. He wanted them to question everything, even if that meant that he was the one being questioned.

Today, Dalí is remembered as one of the most important Surrealist artists.

The Philadelphia Museum of Art held a celebration for the 100th anniversary of Dalí's birth. The exhibition included everything from paintings to furniture, such as **Mae West's Lips Sofa.**

Dalí worked as an artist for more than 60 years. He was always active in the art world. And, Dalí always found himself surrounded by excitement. His **unique** ideas and hard work earned him a place in the history of art.

Timeline

1904 ~ On May 11, Salvador Felipe Jacinto Dalí y Domènech was born in Figueres, Spain.

1918 ~ Dalí had the first public showing of his work.

1924 ~ Dalí was jailed from May 14 to June 12.

1925 ~ Dalí had his first professional solo exhibition.

1928 ~ In March, Dalí released the "Yellow Manifesto."

1929 ~ *An Andalusian Dog* was released.

1930 ~ *The Golden Age* was released and banned in France.

1936 ~ Dalí participated in the First International Surrealist Exhibition; Dalí was featured on the cover of *Time* magazine.

1940 ~ Dalí wrote *The Secret Life of Salvador Dalí*.

1949 ~ Dalí painted *The Madonna of Port Lligat*.

1958 ~ Dalí painted *The Sistine Madonna*.

1974 ~ On September 28, the Dalí Theatre-Museum opened in Figueres.

1989 ~ On January 23, Dalí died.

Fun Facts

- Salvador Dalí began his lifelong interest in costumes around the time he started school. At that young age, he wore a sailor suit and silver-buttoned shoes. And, he carried a cane! At the Residencia, Dalí and his school friends often went out dressed in elaborate costumes. Later, Dalí had a costume that included a cape and a crown.

- In the early 1920s, Dalí experimented with Cubism. Cubists paint images that are broken down into basic shapes. The images look flat, but they are recognizable.

- Dalí told one audience not to worry if they couldn't figure out the meaning of *The Persistence of Memory*. He claimed not to understand it either.

- In 1945, Dalí worked with British director Alfred Hitchcock on the movie *Spellbound*. However, the scene Dalí created for the film was eventually taken out.

Family

Salvador Felipe Jacinto Dalí y Domènech was born on May 11, 1904, in Figueres, Spain. Salvador was the second child in the Dalí family. The first had died just over nine months earlier, at the age of 21 months. He had also been named Salvador. A sister, Ana María, was born in 1906.

Salvador's mother was Felipa Domènech. His father was Don Salvador Dalí y Cusí. Don Salvador made a good living as a **notary** in Spain. The family lived in an area of the country called Catalonia. The Catalonian region has a strong **culture**, including its own language.

According to Salvador, he was sent to a public school at the age of four. His father had to drag him through the streets, kicking and screaming, to get him to go!

However, his father felt Salvador wasn't learning enough at the school. So from ages 6 to 12, Salvador attended the Colegio Hermanos de las Escuelas Cristianas.

The Catalonian region includes the rocky landscape of Cape Creus, which is on Spain's northeast coast. Dalí was inspired by this region, so it appears in many of his works.

A Young Artist

During the summers, the Dalí family lived in Cadaqués, Spain. Throughout his career, Salvador painted scenes from this beautiful area. He often used the local bays, rocks, and coastlines as backgrounds in his paintings.

As a young boy, Salvador showed artistic talent. Later in life, he claimed that he became an artist as soon as he could hold a pencil! Others say he began to paint when he was around eight years old. While in Cadaqués, Salvador took art lessons from Ramón Pitxot, a family friend. Pitxot painted in the **Impressionist** style, which influenced Salvador's early artwork.

By age 13, Salvador was attending the Figueres Institute High School. At the same time, he was attending the Marist Brothers' College. In summer 1918, Salvador had the first public showing of his work. It took place in the lobby of the Municipal Theatre in Figueres. In January 1919, he showed his work there again.

The early influence of Impressionism is evident in Dalí's painting
Port Alguer, Cadaqués. *Impressionist artists worked to create realistic*
representations of color and light in their art.

In 1921, Salvador's mother died of cancer. Salvador was only 17 years old. The same year, he graduated from the Instituto General y Técnico in Figueres.

Dalí then lived at the Residencia de Estudiantes and studied art at the San Fernando Academy in Madrid. There, he met two artists who would become influential in his life. One was filmmaker Luis Buñuel. The other was poet Federico García Lorca.

While studying in Madrid, Salvador was consumed with work. He spent Sundays copying other artists' paintings at the Prado, the national museum of Spain. He also found time to produce a small art newspaper with several other students.

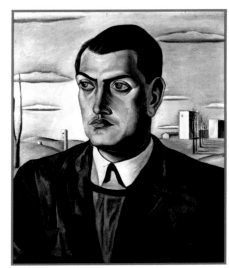

Dalí painted this portrait of his friend Luis Buñuel in 1924.

In 1924, the Spanish government was led by King Alfonso XIII. Among other things, the government was trying to ban the Catalan language. Because his father opposed the government, Salvador was unfairly arrested. He was in prison from May 14 to June 12. When the charges were dropped, Salvador returned to Figueres as a local hero.

Dalí is also known for creating artwork for advertisements. He designed this advertisement for Isotta cars in the mid-1920s.

Surrealism

In 1925, Dalí had his first professional solo exhibition. It was held at the Dalmau Gallery, an important modern art gallery in Barcelona, Spain. The following year, he visited Paris, France, with Ana María and their new stepmother, Catalina. While there, Dalí met the famous artist Pablo Picasso. Picasso liked Dalí's work.

Dalí then returned to Spain. During final examinations in 1926, Dalí declared himself too good to be judged by his teachers. So, he was **expelled** from the San Fernando Academy on June 14.

After being expelled, Dalí returned to Cadaqués and Figueres. He worked to improve his painting **technique**. In 1927, he painted *Neo-Cubist Academy*. This important work shows Dalí's early interest in Surrealism.

Opposite page: Girl Standing at the Window *was included in Dalí's Dalmau Gallery exhibition. The portrait is of his sister, Ana María.*

Barcelona

In 1927, Dalí spent nine months serving in the military. That same year, García Lorca's production of *Mariana Pineda* was performed in Barcelona. Dalí had created the costumes and the set design for the show.

In March 1928, Dalí published the "Yellow Manifesto." Dalí, art **critic** Sebastià Gasch, and literary critic Lluís Montanyà wrote the paper to young Catalans. In it, they condemned traditional Catalan **culture** and defended modernity in art.

The same year, Dalí wanted to participate in an annual showing in Barcelona. But, Dalí's work was becoming more **controversial**. He was pushing the limits of what society would accept as art. So, two works Dalí submitted were rejected.

Artist's Corner

Dalí is most often associated with the Surrealist movement. Poet Isidore Ducasse said Surrealism was "as beautiful as the chance encounter of a sewing machine and an umbrella on a dissecting table." Ducasse is focusing on one of the main ideas behind the movement. Surrealist art often involves seemingly unrelated things combined in unexpected ways.

Dalí's *Burning Giraffe (right)* is a good example of the ideas he brought to the Surrealist movement. There is a giraffe on fire in the background. And, the main human figure has drawers coming out of her body. To Dalí, the drawers symbolized memories. Even though the images in the painting are combined in odd ways, they all remain recognizable and somewhat realistic.

Making a Movie

Dalí's friend Buñuel wanted to create the first Surrealist film. He and Dalí developed an idea that came from things they had dreamed. They wrote the script in six days. Dalí went to Paris to help with the film. It was called *Un Chien Andalou*, or *An Andalusian Dog*. The final film was about 17 minutes long.

Buñuel was very worried about public reaction to the film. At the opening in 1929, he carried stones in his pockets. He was going to use them to defend himself if the audience didn't like it! Luckily, the film's release was a success. It ran for eight months in Paris.

Dalí returned home to Cadaqués for the summer of 1929. Many of his friends joined him there. His guests included Surrealist painter René Magritte and his wife Georgette Berger, as well as Buñuel. Poet Paul Éluard, his wife Helena Deluvina Diakonoff, and their daughter also joined them.

Opposite page: *Dalí worked on several films. This work is from a short animated Surrealist film he created with Walt Disney called* **Destino**.

Gala

Helena Deluvina Diakonoff went by the name Gala. She was Russian and nine years older than Dalí. Usually, Dalí was uncomfortable around women. But, he enjoyed being with Gala.

Dalí continued to challenge traditional art forms. He began to experiment with optical illusions. *Swans Reflecting Elephants* is one of his famous double images. Dalí strove to create double images that were illusions, but still complete objects.

Dalí was also working on a theory he called "paranoiac critical." This idea suggested that people should create their own concept of reality. Dalí expressed this theory through his artwork and personality.

Meanwhile, the romance between Dalí and Gala created problems with his friends and family.

Dalí painted Gala many times.

Optical Illusions

Besides Surrealism, Dalí also experimented with various forms of optical illusions. He sometimes created images that seem to change from one object to another.

Swans Reflecting Elephants (below), is an example of an optical illusion. At first glance, the image is a typical Dalí setting. The background is a port on the rocky Spanish coastline seen in so many of his works. The swans near the water's edge are painted in a realistic manner. Their reflections are correct. However, the reflections are elephants at the same time! This is just one example of the way Dalí was able to use a single image to show two complete objects.

Buñuel felt that Gala was a distraction. And, Dalí's father was angry because Gala was married.

Dalí ignored these objections. So, his father banned him from the whole town and passersby ignored him. Eventually, Dalí and Gala bought a small cottage in Port Lligat, near Cadaqués. Dalí lived there off and on for the rest of his life.

Crossing the Ocean

Encouraged by the success of *An Andalusian Dog*, Dalí and Buñuel made a second Surrealist movie. It was called *L'Age D'Or*, or *The Golden Age*. It began showing on November 28, 1930. The film was longer than *An Andalusian Dog*, running 63 minutes. It was just as shocking and even more **controversial**.

Despite some progress, there was still public resistance to Surrealist art. On December 3, a group called the Patriot's League broke into a viewing of the film. They destroyed Surrealist paintings that were in the lobby. However, Surrealism was gaining some popularity. So, the audience stayed to watch the rest of the film. But by December 11, the film was completely banned in France.

The following year, Dalí finished *The Persistence of Memory*. This painting includes images of melting watches. It is one of his most well-known paintings. Later, the work was bought by the Museum of Modern Art in New York City, New York.

The Persistence of Memory (left) *has been reproduced in countless ways. Dalí re-created it as a sculpture* **(right)**. *And today, there are even real watches and clocks that resemble Dalí's original creation.*

By this time, Gala and Éluard had divorced. So, Dalí and Gala married on January 30, 1934. That autumn, the people of Catalonia revolted against the Spanish government. Dalí and Gala worried about civil war. So, they fled back to France. Once there, a friend helped them leave Europe. Later, the three sailed together to New York City.

More Success

Until the 1930s, Surrealism had been a European art movement. Americans did not know much about it. But the movement was growing. By January 20, 1935, Dalí had sold 12 works and given five lectures in the United States.

After helping popularize Surrealism in New York, Dalí went to London, England. There, the First International Surrealist Exhibition opened in 1936.

At the exhibition, Dalí gave a speech. He came dressed in a diving suit! He held a pool cue in one hand. The leashes to two white Russian wolfhounds were in the other. This presentation delighted the audience and furthered the Surrealist movement's popularity.

Dalí returned to New York a star. On December 14, 1936, *Time* magazine put a portrait of Dalí on its cover. The value of Dalí's work was increasing. And, he was hired to work on storefront

displays, costume design for fashion photography, and a pavilion at a world's fair.

Dalí and Gala also attended a *Bal Onirique*, or "Dreamlike Ball," which was held in their honor. People were asked to come dressed as a dream they had had. Some of the outfits at this Surrealist costume party were as **controversial** as Dalí's paintings.

Dalí and Gala became known for their creative costumes.

Atomic Separation

Life was changing for Dalí. By 1936, the **Spanish Civil War** had begun. Dalí's closest friend, García Lorca, was **assassinated** because of his beliefs. This death haunted Dalí for the rest of his life.

Like García Lorca, Dalí had strong political beliefs. Others in the Surrealist movement disagreed with some political statements he had made. So in 1939, Dalí was **expelled** from the movement.

In May 1940, Dalí and Gala were invited to Virginia. While there, Dalí wrote his **memoir**, *The Secret Life of Salvador Dalí*. Soon after, he declared that he was finished with Surrealism. He said that he would begin adding classical themes into his works.

Dalí had always been interested in modern science. After an **atomic** bomb was dropped during **World War II**, he started a new painting theme. He called it "nuclear painting." Objects in his paintings became separated. They floated above the ground like atomic particles.

By 1948, many artists were being hired to produce religious works. Dalí joined the trend in his **unique** way. His first major work with religious symbols was created in 1949. It is titled *The Madonna of Port Lligat*. And Gala appears in it as the Madonna.

Dalí completed this "nuclear painting" of Gala in 1952. Galatea of the Spheres divides a classical image into particles, showing Dalí's fascination with modern science.

Reinventions

After reinventing his artistic style, Dalí visited Pope Pius XII. He wanted to present his paintings and gain approval for his marriage to Gala. In 1958, Dalí and Gala re-married in a private ceremony. The same year, Dalí painted *The Sistine Madonna*.

During the 1960s, Dalí had more assignments. He worked in Port Lligat and took trips to New York and Paris. In 1970, one of his masterpieces was completed. It was called *The Hallucinogenic Toreador*.

The value of Dalí's paintings had risen dramatically over the years. Now, Dalí decided to build a museum to hold his artwork. The Municipal Theatre in Figueres had been bombed during the **Spanish Civil War**. With Dalí's support, it was reconstructed. On September 28, 1974, it officially became the Dalí Theatre-Museum.

On June 10, 1982, Gala died. After her death, Dalí's health began to fail. His last painting, *The Swallow's Tail*, was completed in 1983. On January 23, 1989, Salvador Dalí passed away.

Surrealist art made many people uncomfortable. It did not look like people thought art should look. Through Dalí's work, Surrealism reached a wide audience. People soon began to appreciate the genre. Thanks to Salvador Dalí, today Surrealist art is valued and respected worldwide.

The Dalí Theatre-Museum in Figueres is the second-most visited museum in Spain. The most visited museum is the Prado, where Dalí spent time during his schooling.

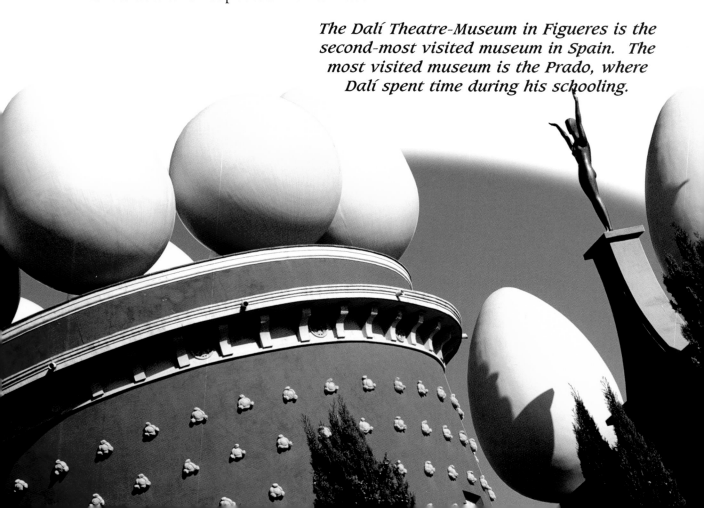

Glossary

assassinate - to murder a very important person, usually for political reasons.

atomic - relating to atoms, the tiny particles that make up elements.

controversial - of or relating to something that causes discussion between groups with strongly different views.

critic - a professional who gives his or her opinion on art or performances.

culture - the customs, arts, and tools of a nation or people at a certain time.

expel - to force out.

Impressionism - an art movement developed by French painters in the late 1800s. They depicted the natural appearances of objects by using strokes or dabs of primary colors.

memoir - a written account of a person's experiences.

notary - a person who specializes in making sure legal documents are real and not forged.

Spanish Civil War - from 1936 to 1939, fought in Spain. The Nationalist forces overthrew the Republican government.

technique - a method or style in which something is done.

unique - being the only one of its kind.

World War II - from 1939 to 1945, fought in Europe, Asia, and Africa. Great Britain, France, the United States, the Soviet Union, and their allies were on one side. Germany, Italy, Japan, and their allies were on the other side.

Saying It

Figueres - fee-GAY-rehs
Luis Buñuel - loo-EES bun-yu-WEHL
memoir - MEHM-wahr

Web Sites

To learn more about Salvador Dalí, visit ABDO Publishing Company on the World Wide Web at **www.abdopublishing.com**. Web sites about Dalí are featured on our Book Links page. These links are routinely monitored and updated to provide the most current information available.

Index